Calvinism's Answer to the Problem of Evil

Stephen Charnock

Monergism Books

Contents

Chapter One

Theodicy & God's Foreknowledge of Sin

Prop. 2. God's holiness is not blemished by enjoining man a law, which he knew he would not observe.

1. Man Created With Original Righteousness.

1. The law was not above his strength. Had the law been impossible to be observed, no crime could have been imputed to the subject, the fault had lain wholly upon the governor; the non-observance of it had been from a want of strength, and not from a want of will. Had God commanded Adam to fly up to the sun, when he had not given him wings, Adam might have a will to obey it, but his power would be too short to perform it. But the law set him for a rule had nothing of impossibility in it; it was easy to be observed; the command was rather below than above his strength, and the sanction of it was more apt to restrain and scare him from the breach of it, than encourage any daring attempts against it. He had as much power, or rather more, to conform to it, than to warp from it; and greater arguments and interest to be

observant of it, than to violate it; his all was secured by the one, and his ruin ascertained by the other.

The commands of God are "not grievous" (1 John 5:3). From the first to the last command there is nothing impossible, nothing hard to the original and created nature of man, which were all summed up in a love to God, which was the pleasure and delight of man, as well as his duty, if he had not by inconsiderateness neglected the dictates and resolves of his own understanding. The law was suited to the strength of man, and fitted for the improvement and perfection of his nature; in which respect the apostle calls it good, as it refers to man; as well as holy, as it refers to God (Rom. 7:12).

Now since God created man a creature capable to be governed by a law, and as a rational creature endued with understanding and will, not to be governed according to his nature without a law, was it congruous to the wisdom of God to respect only the future state of man, which, from the depth of his infinite knowledge, he did infallibly foresee would be miserable by the willful defection of man from the rule? Had it been agreeable to the wisdom of God to respect only this future state, and not the present state of the creature, and therefore leave him lawless, because he knew he would violate the law? Should God forbear to act like a wise governor, because he foresaw that man would cease to act like an obedient subject? Shall a righteous magistrate forbear to make just and good laws, because he foresees, either from the dispositions of his subjects, their ill-humour, or some circumstances which will intervene, that multitudes of them will incline to break those laws, and fall under the penalty of them? No blame can be upon that magistrate who minds the rule of righteousness, and the necessary duty of his government, since he is not the cause of those turbulent affections in men, which he wisely foresees will rise up against his just edicts.

2. Man is Guilty For His Rebellion, Not God.

2. Though the law now be above the strength of man, yet is not the holiness of God blemished by keeping it up. It is true, God hath been graciously pleased to mitigate the severity and rigour of the law by the entrance of the gospel; yet, where men refuse the terms of the gospel, they continue themselves under the condemnation of the law, and are justly guilty of the breach of it, though they have no strength to observe it. The law, as I said before, was not above man's strength, when he was possessed of original righteousness, though it be above man's strength, since he was stripped of original righteousness. The command was dated before man had contracted his impotency, when he had a power to keep it as well as to break it. Had it been enjoined to man only after the fall, and not before, he might have had a better pretense to excuse himself, because of the impossibility of it; yet he would not have had sufficient excuse, since the impossibility did not result from the nature of the law, but from the corrupted nature of the creature. It was "weak through the flesh" (Rom. 8:3), but it was promulged when man had a strength proportioned to the commands of it.

And now, since man hath unhappily made himself incapable of obeying it, must God's holiness in his law be blemished for enjoining it? Must he abrogate those commands, and prohibit what before he enjoined, for the satisfaction of the corrupted creature? Would not this be his ceasing to be holy, that his creature might be unblameably unrighteous? Must God strip himself of his holiness, because man will not discharge his iniquity? He cannot be the cause of sin, by keeping up the law, who would be the cause of all the unrighteousness of men, by removing the authority of it. Some things in the law, that are intrinsically good in their own nature, are indispensable, and it is repugnant to the nature of God not to command them. If he were not the guardian of his indispensable law, he would be the cause and countenancer of the creature's iniquity; so little reason have men to charge God with being the cause of their sin, by not repealing his law to gratify their impotence, that he would be unholy if he did. God must not lose his purity, because man hath lost his; and cast away the right of his sovereignty, because man hath cast away his power of obedience.

3. God's Foreknowledge of the Fall.

3. God's foreknowledge that his law would not be observed lays no blame upon him. Though the foreknowledge of God be infallible, yet it doth not necessitate the creature in acting. It was certain from eternity, that Adam would fall, that men would do such and such actions, that Judas would betray our Saviour; God foreknew all those things from eternity; but it is as certain that this foreknowledge did not necessitate the will of Adam, or any other branch of his posterity, in the doing those actions that were so foreseen by God; they voluntarily run into such courses, not by any impulsion. God's knowledge was not suspended between certainty and uncertainty. He certainly foreknew that his law would be broken by Adam; he foreknew it in his own decree of not hindering him, by giving Adam the efficacious grace which would infallibly have prevented it; yet Adam did freely break this law, and never imagined that the foreknowledge of God did necessitate him to it. He could find no cause of his own sin but the liberty of his own will; he charges the occasion of his sin upon the woman, and consequently upon God in giving the woman to him (Gen. 3:12). He could not be so ignorant of the nature of God as to imagine him without a foresight of future things, since his knowledge of what was to be known of God by creation was greater than any man's since, in all probability.

But, however, if he were not acquainted with the notion of God's foreknowledge, he could not be ignorant of his own act; there could not have been any necessity upon him, any kind of constraint of him in his action that could have been unknown to him; and he would not have omitted a plea of so strong a nature, when he was upon his trial for life or death, especially when he urgeth so weak an argument to impute his crime to God as the gift of the woman, as if that which was designed him for a help were intended for his ruin.

If God's prescience takes away the liberty of the creature, there is no such thing as a free action in the world (for there is nothing done but is foreknown by God, else we render God of a limited understanding), nor ever was, no, not by God himself ad extra; for whatsoever he hath done in creation, whatsoever he hath done since the creation, was foreknown by him; he resolved to do it, and therefore foreknew that he would do it. Did God do it therefore necessarily, as necessity is opposed to liberty? As he freely decrees what he will do, so he effects what he freely decreed. Foreknowledge is so far from entrenching upon the liberty of the will, that predetermination, which in the notion of it speaks something more, doth not dissolve it; God did not only foreknow, but determine the suffering of Christ (Acts 4:27-28).

It was necessary, therefore, that Christ should suffer, that God might not be mistaken in his foreknowledge, or come short of his determinate decree. But did this take away the liberty of Christ in suffering? "Who offered himself up to God" (Eph. 5:2), that is, by a voluntary act, as well as designed to do it by a determinate counsel. It did infallibly secure the event, but did not annihilate the liberty of the action, either in Christ's willingness to suffer, or the crime of the Jews that made him suffer. God's prescience is God's prevision of things arising from their proper causes; as a gardener foresees in his plants the leaves and the flowers that will arise from them in the spring, because he knows the strength and nature of their several roots which lie under ground, but his foresight of these things is not the cause of the rise and appearance of those flowers. If any of us see a ship moving towards such a rock or quicksand, and know it to be governed by a negligent pilot, we shall certainly foresee that the ship will be torn in pieces by the rock, or swallowed up by the sands; but is this foresight of ours from the causes, any cause of the effect, or can we from hence be said to be the authors of the miscarriage of the ship, and the loss of the passengers and goods?

The fall of Adam was foreseen by God to come to pass by the consent of his free will in the choice of the proposed temptation. God foreknew Adam would sin, and if Adam would not have sinned, God would have foreknown that he would not sin. Adam might easily have detected the serpent's fraud, and made a better election; God foresaw that he would not do it; God's foreknowledge did not make Adam guilty or innocent; whether God had foreknown it or no, he was guilty by a free choice, and a willing neglect of his own duty. Adam knew that God foreknew that he might eat of the fruit, and fall and die, because God had forbidden him; the foreknowledge that he would do it was no more a cause of his action than the foreknowledge that he might do it. Judas certainly knew that his master foreknew that he should betray him, for Christ had acquainted him with it (John 13:21, 26), yet he never charged this foreknowledge of Christ with any guilt of his treachery.

Chapter Two

Theodicy & God's Decree of Reprobation

Prop. 3. The holiness of God is not blemished by decreeing the eternal rejection of some men.

Reprobation in its first notion is an act of preterition, or passing by. A man is not made wicked by the act of God, but it supposeth him wicked, and so it is nothing else but God's leaving a man in that guilt and filth wherein he beholds him. In its second notion it is an ordination, not to a crime, but to a punishment—an ordaining to condemnation (Jude 4). And though it be an eternal act of God, yet in order of nature it follows upon the foresight of the transgression of man, and supposeth the crime. God considers Adam's revolt, and views the whole mass of his corrupted posterity, and chooses some to reduce to himself by his grace, and leaves others to lie sinking in their ruins. Since all mankind fell by the fall of Adam, and have corruption conveyed to them successively by that root whereof they are branches; all men might justly be left wallowing in that miserable condition to which they were reduced by the apostasy of their common head, and God might have passed by the whole race of man, as well as he did the fallen angels, without any hope of redemption.

He was no more bound to restore man than to restore devils, nor bound to repair the nature of any one son of Adam; and had he dealt with men as he dealt with the devils, they had had all of them as little just ground to complain of God; for all men deserved to be left to themselves, for all were "concluded under sin" (Gal. 3:22). But God calls out some to make monuments of his grace, which is an act of the sovereign mercy of that dominion whereby "he hath mercy on whom he will have mercy" (Rom. 9:18). Others he passes by, and leaves them remaining in that corruption of nature wherein they were born. If men have a power to dispose of their own goods, without any unrighteousness, why should not God dispose of his own grace, and bestow it upon whom he pleases, since it is a debt to none, but a free gift to any that enjoy it?

God is not the cause of sin in this, because his operation about this is negative; it is not an action, but a denial of action, and therefore cannot be the cause of the evil actions of men. God acts nothing, but withholds his power; he doth not enlighten their minds, nor incline their wills so powerfully as to expel their darkness, and root out those evil habits which possess them by nature. God could, if he would, savingly enlighten the minds of all men in the world, and quicken their hearts with a new life by an invincible grace, but in not doing it there is no positive act of God, but a cessation of action. We may with as much reason say, that God is the cause of all the sinful actions that are committed by the corporation of devils since their first rebellion, because he leaves them to themselves, and bestows not a new grace upon them; as say God is the cause of the sins of those that he overlooks and leaves in that state of guilt wherein he found them. God did not pass by any without the consideration of sin, so that this act of God is not repugnant to his holiness, but conformable to his justice.

Chapter Three

Theodicy & God's Permission of Sin

P rop. 4. The holiness of God is not blemished by his secret will to suffer sin to enter into the world. God never willed sin by his preceptive will. It was never founded upon, or produced by any word of his, as the creation was. He never said, "Let there be sin under the heaven," as he said, "Let there be water under the heaven" (Gen. 1:9). Nor doth he will it by infusing any habit of it, or stirring up inclinations to it; no, "God tempts no man" (James 1:13). Nor doth he will it by his approving will; it is detestable to him, nor ever can be otherwise. He cannot approve it either before commission or after.

1. The will of God is in some sort concurrent with sin.

He doth not properly will it, but he wills not to hinder it, to which by his omnipotence he could put a bar. If he did positively will it, it might be wrought by himself, and so could not be evil. If he did in no sort will it, it would not be committed by his creature. Sin entered into the world, either God willing the permission of it, or not willing the permission of it. The latter cannot be said, for then the creature is more powerful than God, and can do that which God will not permit.

God can, if he be pleased, banish all sin in a moment out of the world; he could have prevented the revolt of angels, and the fall of man, they did not sin whether he would or no; he might by his grace have stepped in the first moment, and made a special impression upon them of the happiness they already possessed, and the misery they would incur by any wicked attempt. He could as well have prevented the sin of the fallen angels, and confirmed them in grace, as of those that continued in their happy state; he might have appeared to man, informed him of the issue of his design, and made secret impressions upon his heart, since he was acquainted with every avenue to his will. God could have kept all sin out of the world, as well as all creatures from breathing in it; he was as well able to bar sin for ever out of the world as to let creatures lie in the womb of nothing, wherein they were first wrapped.

To say God doth will sin as he doth other things, is to deny his holiness; to say it entered without anything of his will, is to deny his omnipotence. If he did necessitate Adam to fall, what shall we think of his purity? If Adam did fall without any concern of God's will in it, what shall we say of his sovereignty? The one taints his holiness, and the other clips his power. If it came without anything of his will in it, and he did not foresee it, where is his omniscience? If it entered whether he would or no, where is his omnipotence? "Who hath resisted his will?" (Rom. 9:19). There cannot he a lustful act in Abimelech if God will withhold his power: "I withheld thee" (Gen. 20:6); nor a cursing word in Balaam's mouth, unless God give power to speak it: "Have I now any power at all to say anything? The word that God puts in my mouth, that shall I speak" (Num. 22:38). As no action could be sinful if God had not forbidden it, so no sin could be committed if God did not will to give way to it.

2. God doth not will sin directly, and by an efficacious will.

He doth not directly will it, because he hath prohibited it by his law, which is a discovery of his will. So that if he should directly will sin, and directly prohibit it, he would will good and evil in the same manner, and there would be contradictions in God's will. To will sin absolutely is to work it. "God hath done whatsoever he pleased." (Ps. 115:3). God cannot absolutely will it, because he cannot work it. God wills good by a *positive decree*, because he hath decreed to effect it. He wills evil by a *privative decree*, because he hath decreed not to give that grace which would certainly prevent it. God doth not will sin simply, for that were to approve it, but he wills it in order to that good his wisdom will bring forth from it. He wills not sin for itself, but for the event.

To will sin as sin, or as purely evil, is not in the capacity of a creature, neither of man nor devil. The will of a rational creature cannot will anything but under the appearance of good, of some good in the sin itself, or some good in the issue of it. Much more is this from God, who being infinitely good, cannot will evil as evil, and being infinitely knowing, cannot will that for good which is evil. Infinite wisdom can be under no error or mistake. To will sin as sin would be an unanswerable blemish on God, but to will to suffer it in order to good is the glory of his wisdom. It could never have peeped up its head unless there had been some decree of God concerning it. And there had been no decree of God concerning it, had he not intended to bring good and glory out of it. If God did directly will the discovery of his grace and mercy to the world, he did in some sort will sin, as that without which there could not have been any appearance of mercy in the world; for an innocent creature is not the object of mercy, but a miserable creature, and no rational creature but must be sinful before it be miserable.

3. God wills the permission of sin.

He doth not positively will sin, but he positively wills to permit it. And though he doth not approve of sin, yet he approves of that act of his will whereby he permits it. For since that sin could not enter into the world without some concern of God's will about it, that act of his will that gave way to it could not be displeasing to him. God could never be displeased with his own act: "He is not a man that he should repent" (1 Sam. 15:29). What God cannot repent of, he cannot but approve of; it is contrary to the blessedness of God to disapprove of, and be displeased with, any act of his own will. If he hated any act of his own will, he would hate himself, he would be under a torture; every one that hates his own acts is under some disturbance and torment for them. That which is permitted by him is in itself, and in regard of the evil of it, hateful to him; but as the prospect of that good which he aims at in the permission of it is pleasing to him, so that act of his will whereby he permits it is ushered in by an approving act of his understanding. Either God approved of the permission or not; if he did not approve his own act of permission, he could not have decreed an act of permission. It is unconceivable that God should decree such an act which he detested, and positively will that which he hated.

Though God hated sin, as being against his holiness, yet he did not hate the permission of sin, as being subservient by the immensity of his wisdom to his own glory. He could never be displeased with that which was the result of his eternal counsel, as this decree of permitting sin was, as well as any other decree resolved upon in his own breast. For as God acts nothing in time, but what he decreed from eternity, so he permits nothing in time, but what he decreed from eternity to permit. To speak properly, therefore, God doth not will sin, but he wills the permission of it, and this will to permit is active and positive in God.

4. This act of permission is not a mere and naked permission, but such an one as is attended with a certainty of the event.

The decrees of God to make use of the sin of man for the glory of his grace, in the mission and passion of his Son, hung upon this entrance of sin; would it consist with the wisdom of God to decree such great and stupendous things, the event whereof should depend upon an uncertain foundation, which he might be mistaken in? God would have sat in council from eternity to no purpose, if he had only permitted those things to be done, without any knowledge of the event of this permission; God would not have made such provision for redemption to no purpose, or an uncertain purpose, which would have been if man had not fallen, or if it had been an uncertainty with God whether he would fall or no. Though the will of God about sin was permissive, yet the will of God about that glory he would promote by the defect of the creature was positive, and therefore, he would not suffer so many positive acts of his will to hang upon an uncertain event, and therefore he did wisely and righteously order all things to the accomplishment of his great and gracious purposes. [1]

5. This act of permission doth not taint the holiness of God.

That there is such an act as permission is clear in Scripture: "Who in times past suffered all nations to walk in their own ways" (Acts 14:16), but that it doth not blemish the holiness of God will appear,

(1) From the nature of this permission.

[1] It is not a moral permission.

It is not a moral permission, a giving liberty of toleration by any law to commit sin with impunity, when what one law did forbid another law doth leave indifferent to be done or not, as a man sees good in himself; as when there is a law made among men, that no man shall go out of a city or country without license, to go without license is a crime by the law; but when that law is repealed by another, that gives liberty for men to go and come at their pleasure, it doth not make their going or coming necessary,

---

1. [1] *cf.* Westminster Confession of Faith 5.4, "The almighty power, unsearchable wisdom, and infinite goodness of God so far manifest themselves in his providence that it extendeth itself even to the first fall, and all other sins of angels and men (2 Sam 16:10; 24:1 with 1 Chr 21:1; 1 Kings 22:22-23; 1 Chr 10:4, 13-14; Acts 2:23; 4:27-28; Rom 11:32-34), and that not by a bare permission (Acts 14:16), but such as hath joined with it a most wise and powerful bounding (2 Kings 19:28; Ps 76:10), and otherwise ordering and governing of them, in a manifold dispensation, to his own holy ends (Gen 50:20; Isa 10:6-7, 12); yet so as the sinfulness thereof proceedeth only from the creature, and not from God; who, being most holy and righteous, neither is nor can be the author or approver of sin (Ps 50:21; James 1:13-14, 17; 1 John 2:16)."

but leaves those which were before bound, to do as they see good in themselves. Such a permission makes a fact lawful, though not necessary; a man is not obliged to do it, but he is left to his own discretion to do as he pleases, without being chargeable with a crime for doing it. Such a permission there was granted by God to Adam of eating of the fruits of the garden, to choose any of them for food, except the tree of knowledge of good and evil. It was a precept to him not to eat of the fruit of the tree of knowledge of good and evil, but the other was a permission, whereby it was lawful for him to feed upon any other that was most agreeable to his appetite. But there is not such a permission in the case of sin; this had been an indulgence of it which had freed man from any crime, and consequently from punishment, because by such a permission by law he would have had authority to sin if he pleased. God did not remove the law which he had before placed as a bar against evil, nor ceased that moral impediment of his threatening; such a permission as this, to make sin lawful or indifferent, had been a blot upon God's holiness.

[2] God's permission is no more than the not hindering a sinful action which he could have prevented.

But this permission of God in the case of sin, is no more than the not hindering a sinful action which he could have prevented. It is not so much an action of God, as a suspension of his influence, which might have hindered an evil act, and a forbearing to restrain the faculties of man from sin; it is properly the not exerting that efficacy which might change the counsels that are taken, and prevent the action intended; as when one man sees another ready to fall, and can preserve him from falling by reaching out his hand, he permits him to fall, that is, he hinders him not from falling: so God describes his act about Abimelech, "I withheld thee from sinning against me, therefore suffered I thee not to touch her" (Gen. 20:6). If Abimelech had sinned, he had sinned by God's permission, that is, by God's not hindering or not restraining him, by making any impressions upon him; so that permission is only a withholding that help and grace, which, if bestowed, would have been an effectual remedy to prevent a crime; and it is rather a suspension or cessation, than properly a permission; and sin may be said to be committed not without, God's permission, rather than by his permission.

Thus in the fall of man, God did not hold the reins strict upon Satan to restrain him from laying the bait, nor restrain Adam from swallowing the bait; he kept to himself that efficacious grace which he might hare darted out upon man to prevent his fall. God left Satan to his malice of tempting, and Adam to his liberty of resisting and his own strength, to use that sufficient grace he had furnished him with, whereby he might have resisted and overcome the temptation. As he did not drive man to it, so he did not secretly restrain him from it. So in the Jews" crucifying our Saviour; God did not imprint upon their minds, by his Spirit, a consideration of the greatness of the crime, and the horror of his justice due to it, and being without those impediments, they run furiously of their own accord to the commission of that evil; as when a man lets a wolf or dog out upon his prey, he takes off the chain which held them, and they presently act according to their natures.

In the fall of angels and men, God's act was a leaving them to their own strength. In sins after the fall, it is God's giving them up to their own corruption. The first is a pure suspension of grace, the other hath the nature of a punishment: "so I gave them up to their own hearts' lust" (Ps. 81:1). The first object of this permissive will of God was to leave angels and men to their own liberty and the use of their free will, which was natural to them, not adding that supernatural grace which was necessary, not that they should not at all sin, but that they should infallibly not sin; they had a strength sufficient to avoid sin, but not sufficient infallibly to avoid sin, a grace sufficient to preserve them, but not sufficient to confirm them.

[3] This permission is not the cause of sin.

Now this permission is not the cause of sin, nor doth blemish the holiness of God; it doth not intrench upon the freedom of men, but supported it, established it, and leaves man to it. God acted nothing, but only ceased to act, and therefore could not be the efficient cause of man's sin. As God is not the author of good but by willing and effecting it, so he is not the author of evil but by willing and effecting it. But he doth not positively will evil, nor effect it by any efficacy of his own. Permission is no action, nor the cause of that action which is permitted, but the will of that person who is permitted to do such an action is the cause. God can no more be said to be the cause of sin, by suffering a creature to act as it will, than be can be said to be the cause of the not being of any creature by denying it being, and letting it remain nothing; it is not from God that it is nothing, it is nothing in itself. Though God be said to be the cause of creation, yet he is never by any said to be the cause of that nothing which was before creation. This permission of God is not the cause of sin, but the cause of not hindering sin. Man and angels had a physical power of sinning from God, as they were created with free will and supported in their natural strength, but the moral power to sin was not from God; he counseled them not to it, laid no obligation upon them to use their natural power for such an end; he only left them to their freedom, and not hindered them in their acting what he was resolved to permit.

(2) The holiness of God is not tainted by this, because he was under no obligation to hinder their commission of sin.

Ceasing to act, whereby to prevent a crime for mischief, brings not a person permitting it under guilt, unless where he is under an obligation to prevent it; but God, in regard of his absolute dominion, cannot be charged with any such obligation. One man that doth not hinder the murder of another when it is in his power, is guilty of the murder in part; but it is to be considered that he is under a tie by nature, as being of the same kind, and being the other's brother by a communion of blood, also under an obligation of the law of charity, enacted by the common sovereign of the world; but what tie was there upon God, since the infinite transcendency of his nature and his sovereign dominion frees him from any such obligation? "If he takes away, who shall say, What dost thou?" (Job 9:12). God might have prevented the fall of men and angels, he might have confirmed them all in a state of perpetual innocency, but where is the obligation? He had made the creature a debtor to himself, but he owed nothing to the creature.

Before God can be charged with any guilt in this case, it must be proved, not only that he could, but that he was bound to hinder it. No person can be justly charged with another's fault merely for not preventing it, unless he be bound to prevent it; else not only the first sin of angels and man would be imputed to God as the author, but all the sins of men. He could not be obliged by any law, because he had no superior to impose any law upon him, and it will be hard to prove that he was obliged from his own nature to prevent the entrance of sin, which he would use as an occasion to declare his own holiness, so transcendent a perfection of his nature, more than ever it could have been manifested by a total exclusion of it, viz., in the death of Christ. He is no more bound in his own nature to preserve, by supernatural grace, his creatures from falling after he had framed them with sufficient strength to stand, than he was obliged in his own nature to bring his creature into being, when it was nothing. He is not bound to create a rational creature, much less bound to create him with supernatural gifts; though, since God would make a rational creature, he could not but make him with a natural, uprightness and rectitude.

God did as much for angels and men as became a wise governor. He had published his law, backed it with severe penalties, and the creature wanted not a natural strength to observe and obey it. Had not man a power to obey all the precepts of the law as well as one? How was God bound to give him more grace, since what he had already was enough to shield him, and keep up his resistance against all the power of hell! It had been enough to have pointed his will against the temptation, and he had kept off the force of it. Was there any promise passed to Adam of any further grace, which he could plead as a tie upon God? No such voluntary limit upon God's supreme dominion appears upon record. Was anything due to man which he had not? anything promised him which was not performed? What action of debt, then, can the creature bring against God?

Indeed, when man began to neglect the light of his own reason, and became inconsiderate of the precept, God might have enlightened his understanding by a special flash, a supernatural beam, and imprinted upon him a particular consideration of the necessity of his obedience, the misery he was approaching to by his sin, the folly of any such apprehension of an equality in knowledge; he might have convinced him of the falsity of the serpent's arguments, and uncased to him the venom that lay under those baits. But how doth it appear that God was bound to those additional acts, when he had already lighted up in him a spirit which was "the candle of the Lord" (Prov. 20:27), whereby he was able to discern all, if he had attended to it.

It was enough that God did not necessitate man to sin, did not counsel him to it, that he had given him sufficient warning in the threatening, and sufficient strength in his faculties, to fortify him against temptation.

He gave him what was due to him as a creature of his own framing, he withdrew no help from him that was due to him as a creature, and what was not due he was not bound to impart. Man did not beg preserving grace of God, and God was not bound to offer it when he was not petitioned for it especially; yet if he had begged it, God having before furnished him sufficiently, might, by the right of his sovereign dominion, have denied it without any impeachment of his holiness and righteousness. Though he would not in such a case have dealt so bountifully with his creature as he might have done, yet he could not have been impleaded as dealing unrighteously with his creature. The single word that God had already uttered when he gave him his precept, was enough to oppose against all the devil's wiles, which tended to invalidate that word. The understanding of man could not imagine that the word of God was vainly spoken; and the very suggestion of the devil, as if the Creator should envy his creature, would have appeared ridiculous if he had attended to the voice of his own reason. God had done enough for him, and was obliged to do no more, and dealt not unrighteously in leaving him to act according to the principles of his nature.

To conclude, If God's permission of sin were enough to charge it upon God, or if God had been obliged to give Adam supernatural grace, Adam, that had so capacious a brain, could not be without that plea in his mouth, Lord, thou mightest have prevented it; the commission of it by me could not have been without thy permission of it; or, Thou hast been wanting to me, as the author of my nature. No such plea is brought by Adam into the court, when God tried and cast him; no such pleas can have any strength in them. Adam had reason enough to know that there was sufficient reason to overrule such a plea.

Since the permission of sin casts no dirt upon the holiness of God, as I think hath been cleared, we may under this head consider two things more.

6. God's permission of sin is not so much as his restraint or limitation of it.

Since the entrance of the first sin into the world by Adam, God is more a hinderer than a permitter of it. If he hath permitted that which he could have prevented, he prevents a world more, that he might, if he pleased, permit. The hedges about sin are larger than the outlets; they are but a few streams that glide about the world, in comparison of that mighty torrent he dams up both in men and devils. He that understands what a lake of Sodom is in every man's nature, since the universal infection of human nature, as the apostle describes it (Rom. 3:9-10), must acknowledge, that if God should cast the reins upon the necks of sinful men, they would ran into thousands of abominable crimes more than they do. The impression of all natural laws would be razed out, the world would be a public stew, and a more bloody slaughter-house; human society would sink into a chaos; no star-light of commendable morality would be seen in it; the world would be no longer an earth, but a hell, and have lain deeper in wickedness than it doth. If God did not limit sin, as he doth the sea, and put bars to the waves of the heart, as well as those of the waters, and say of them, "Hitherto you shall go, and no further," man hath such a furious ocean in him, as would overflow the banks; and where it makes a breach in one place, it would in a thousand, if God should suffer it to act according to its impetuous current.

The devil hath lust enough to destroy all mankind, if God did not bridle him; deal with every man as he did with Job, ruin their comforts, and deform their bodies with scabs; infect religion with a thousand more errors; fling disorders into commonwealths, and make them as a fiery furnace, full of nothing but flame. If he were not chained by that powerful arm, that might let him loose to fulfill his malicious fury, what rapines, murders, thefts, would be committed, if he did not stint him! Abimelech would not only lust after Sarah, but deflower her; Laban not only pursue Jacob, but rifle him; Saul not only hate David, but murder him; David not only threaten Nabal, but root him up, and his family, did not God restrain the wrath of man (Ps. 76:10). A greater remainder of wrath is pent in, than flames out, which yet swells for an outlet. God may be concluded more holy in preventing men's sins, than the author of sin in permitting some; since, were it not for his restraints, by the pull-back of conscience, and infused motions and outward impediments, the world would swarm more with this cursed brood.

7. His permission of sin is in order to his own glory and a greater good.

It is no reflection upon the divine goodness to leave man to his own conduct, whereby such a deformity as sin sets foot in the world; since he makes his wisdom illustrious in bringing good out of evil, and a good greater than that evil he suffered to spring up. God did not permit sin, as sin, or permit it barely for itself. As sin is not lovely in its own nature, so neither is the permission of sin intrinsically good or amiable for itself, but for those ends aimed at in the permission of it. God permitted sin, but approved not of the object of that permission, sin; because that, considered in its own nature, is solely evil: nor can we think that God could approve of the act of permission, considered only in itself as an act, but as it respected that event which his wisdom would order by it.

We cannot suppose that God should permit sin, but for some great and glorious end; for it is the manifestation of his own glorious perfections he intends in all the acts of his will: "The Lord hath made all things for himself" (Prov. 16:4)—hath wrought ( )□□□□all things, which is not only his act of creation, but ordination; for himself, that is, for the discovery of the excellency of his nature, and the communication of himself to his creature. Sin, indeed, in its own nature, hath no tendency to a good end; the womb of it teems with nothing but monsters; it is a spurn at God's sovereignty, and a slight of his goodness. It both deforms and torments the person that acts it; it is black and abominable, and hath not a mite of goodness in the nature of it. If it ends in any good, it is only from that infinite transcendency of skill that can bring good out of evil, as well as light out of darkness.

Therefore God did not permit it as sin, but as it was an occasion for the manifestation of his own glory. Though the goodness of God would have appeared in the preservation of the world, as well as it did in the creation of it, yet his mercy could not have appeared without the entrance of sin, because the object of mercy is a miserable creature; but man could not be miserable as long as he remained innocent. The reign of sin opened a door for the reign and triumph of grace: "As sin hath reigned unto death, so might grace reign through righteousness to eternal life" (Rom. 5:21).

Without it, the bowels of mercy had never sounded, and the ravishing music of divine grace could never have been heard by the creature. Mercy, which renders God so amiable, could never else have beamed out to the world. Angels and men upon this occasion beheld the stirrings of divine grace, and the tenderness of divine nature, and the glory of the divine persons in their several functions about the redemption of man, which had else been a spring shut up and a fountain sealed; the song of "Glory to God, and goodwill to men" (Luke 2:14), in a way of redemption, had never been sung by them.

It appears in his dealings with Adam, that he permitted his fall, not only to shew his justice in punishing, but principally his mercy in rescuing; since he proclaims to him first the promise of a Redeemer to bruise the serpent's head, before he settled the punishment he should smart under in the world (Gen. 3:15-17). And what fairer prospect could the creature have of the holiness of God, and his hatred of sin, than in the edge of that sword of justice which punished it in the sinner, but glittered more in the punishment of a surety so near allied to him? Had not man been criminal, he could not have been punishable, nor any been punishable for him; and the pulse of divine holiness could not have beaten so quick, and been so visible, without an exercise of his vindicative justice. He left man's mutable nature to fall under unrighteousness, that thereby he might commend the righteousness of his own nature (Rom. 3:7).

Adam's sin in its nature tended to the ruin of the world, and God takes an occasion from it for the glory of his grace in the redemption of the world. He brings forth thereby a new scene of wonders from heaven, and a surprising knowledge on earth: as the sun breaks out more strongly after a night of darkness and tempest. As God in creation framed a chaos by his power, to manifest his wisdom in bringing order out of disorder, light out of darkness, beauty out of confusion and deformity, when he was able by a word to have made all creatures to stand up in their beauty, without the precedency of a chaos: so God permitted a moral chaos, to manifest a greater wisdom in the repairing a broken image, and restoring a deplorable creature, and bringing out those perfections of his nature, which had else been wrapt up in a perpetual silence in his bosom. It was therefore very congruous to the holiness of God, to permit that which he could make subservient for his own glory, and particularly for the manifestation of this attribute of holiness, which seems to be in opposition to such a permission.

Chapter Four

Theodicy &
The Concurrence
of Primary &
Secondary Causes

"God from all eternity did, by the most wise and holy counsel of his own will, freely and unchangeably ordain whatsoever comes to pass (Rom 9:15, 18; 11:33; Eph 1:11; Heb 6:17); yet so as thereby neither is God the author of sin (James 1:13, 17; 1 John 1:5), nor is violence offered to the will of the creatures, nor is the liberty or contingency of second causes taken away, but rather established (Prov 16:33; Mat 17:12; John 19:11; Acts 2:23; 4:27-28)." (Westminster Confession of Faith 3.2).

Prop. 5. The holiness of God is not blemished by his concurrence with the creature in the material part of a sinful act. Some, to free God from having any hand in sin, deny his concurrence to the actions of the creature; because, if he concurs to a sinful action, he concurs to the sin also: not understanding how there can be a distinction between the act and the sinfulness or viciousness of it, and how God can concur to a natural action, without being stained by that moral evil which cleaves to it. For the understanding of this, observe:

1. God's concurrence with the creature.

There is a concurrence of God to all the acts of the creature: "In him we live, and move, and have our being" (Acts 17:28). We depend upon God in our acting as well as in our being. There is as much an efficacy of God in our motion as in our production—as none have life without his power in producing it, so none have any operation without his providence concurring with it. "In him," or "by him," that is, by his virtue preserving and governing our motions, as well by his power bringing as into being. Hence man is compared to an ax (Isa. 10:15), an instrument that hath no action without the cooperation of a superior agent handling it. The actions of the second causes are ascribed to God. The grass, that is the product of the sun, rain, and earth, he is said to make to grow upon the mountains (Ps. 147:8), and the skin and flesh, which is by natural generation, he is said to clothe us with (Job. 10:5), in regard of his co-working with second causes, according to their natures.

Nothing can exist or operate without God.

As nothing can exist, so nothing can operate without him. Let his concurrence be removed, and the being and action of the creature would cease. Remove the sun from the horizon, or a candle from a room, and the light which floweth from either of them ceaseth. Without God's preserving and concurring power, the course of nature would sink, and the creation be in vain. All created things depend upon God as agents, as well as beings, and are subordinate to him in a way of action, as well as in a way of existing. If God suspends his influence from their action, they would cease to act (as the fire did from burning the three children), as well as if God suspends his influence from their being, they would cease to be.

God supports the nature whereby actions are wrought, the mind where actions are consulted, and the will where actions are determined, and the motive power whereby actions are produced. The mind could not contrive, nor the hand act a wickedness, if God did not support the power of the one in designing, and the strength of the other in executing a wicked intention. Every faculty in its being, and every faculty in its motion, hath a dependence upon the influence of God. To make the creature independent upon God in anything which speaks perfection—as action considered as action is—is to make a creature a sovereign being. Indeed, we cannot imagine the concurrence of God to the good actions of men since the Fall, without granting a concurrence of God to evil actions, because there is no action so purely good, but hath a mixture of evil in it, though it takes its denomination of good from the better part: "There is no man that doeth good and sins not" (Eccles. 7:20).

2. Concurrence does not mar God's holiness.

Though the natural virtue of doing a sinful action be from God, and supported by him, yet this doth not blemish the holiness of God. While God concurs with them in the act, he instills no evil into men.

(1) No act in regard of the substance of it is evil.

Most of the actions of our faculties, as they are actions, might have been in the state of innocency. Eating is an act Adam would have used if he had stood firm, but not eating to excess. Worship was an act that should have been performed to God in innocence, but not hypocritically. Every action is good by a physical goodness, as it is an act of the mind or hand, which have a natural goodness by creation, but every action is not morally good. The physical goodness of the action depends on God, the moral evil on the creature.

There is no action, as a corporeal action, is prohibited by the law of God, but as it springs from an evil disposition, and is tainted by a venomous temper of mind. There is no action so bad, as attended with such objects and circumstances, but if the objects and circumstances were changed might be a brave and commendable action. So that the moral goodness or badness of an act is not to be esteemed from the substance of the act, which hath always a physical goodness, but from the objects, circumstances, and constitution of the mind in the doing of it. Worship is an act good in itself, but the worship of an image is bad in regard of the object. Were that act of worship directed to God that is paid to a statue, and offered up to him with a sincere frame of mind, it would be morally good. The act in regard of the substance is the same in both, and considered as separated from the object to which the worship is directed, hath the same real goodness in regard of its substance. But when you consider this action in relation to the different objects, the one hath a moral goodness, and the other a moral evil.

Example: Speaking.

So in speaking. Speaking, being a motion of the tongue in the forming of words, is an excellency belonging to a reasonable creature, an endowment bestowed, continued, and supported by God. Now if the same tongue forms words whereby it curseth God this minute, and forms words whereby it blesses and praises God the next minute, the faculty of speaking is the same, the motion of the tongue is the same in pronouncing the name of God either in a way of cursing or blessing: it is the "same mouth that blesseth and curseth" (James 3:9-10). The motion of it is naturally good in regard of the substance of the act in both. It is the use of an excellent power God hath given, and which God preserves in the use of it. But the estimation of the moral goodness or evil is not from the act itself, but from the disposition of the mind.

Example: Killing.

Once more, killing as an act is good, nor is it unlawful as an act; for if so, God would never have commanded his people Israel to wage any war, and justice could not be done upon malefactors by the magistrate. A man were bound to sacrifice his life to the fury of an invader, rather than secure it by despatching that of an enemy. But killing an innocent, or killing without authority, or out of revenge, is bad. It is not the material part of the act, but the object, manner, and circumstance that makes it good or evil. It is no blemish to God's holiness to concur to the substance of an action, without having any hand in the immorality of it, because whatsoever is real in the substance of the action might be done without evil. It is not evil as it is an act, as it is a motion of the tongue or hand, for then every motion of the tongue or hand would be evil.

(2) Actions in themselves vs. actions as evil.

Hence it follows that an act as an act is one thing, and the viciousness another. The action is the efficacy of the faculty, extending itself to some outward object; but the sinfulness of an act consists in a privation of that comeliness and righteousness which ought to be in an action, in a want of conformity of the act with the law of God, either written in nature or revealed in the word. Now the sinfulness of an action is not the act itself, but is considered in it as it is related to the law, and is a deviation from it. And so the sinfulness is something cleaving to the action, and therefore to be distinguished from the act itself, which is the subject of the sinfulness. When we say such an action is sinful, the action is the subject and the sinfulness of the action is that which adheres to it. The action is not the sinfulness, nor the sinfulness the action. They are distinguished as the member and a disease in the member, the arm and the palsy in it. The arm is not the palsy, nor is the palsy the arm; but the palsy is a disease that cleaves to the arm. So sinfulness is a deformity that cleaves to an action.

The evil of an action is not the effect of an action, nor attends it as it is an action, but as it is an action so circumstantiated and conversant about this or that object; for the same action done by two several persons may be good in one and bad in the other—-as when two judges are in joint commission for the trial of a malefactor, both upon the appearance of his guilt condemn him. This action in both, considered as an action, is good, for it is an adjudging a man to death whose crime deserves such a punishment. But this same act, which is but one joint act of both, may be morally good in one judge and morally evil in the other: morally good in him that condemns him out of an unbiased consideration of the demerit of his fact, obedience to the law, and conscience of the duty of his place; and morally evil in the other, who hath no respect to those considerations, but joins in the act of condemnation, principally moved by some private animosity against the prisoner, and desire of revenge for some injury he hath really received, or imagines that he hath received from him. The act in itself is the same materially in both; but in one it is an act of justice, and in the other an act of murder, as it respects the principles and motives of it in the two judges; take away the respect of private revenge, and the action in the ill judge had been as laudable as the action of the other.

The substance of an act and the sinfulness of an act are separable and distinguishable. God may concur with the substance of an act without concurring with the sinfulness of the act. As the good judge, that condemned the prisoner out of conscience, concurred with the evil judge who condemned the prisoner out of private revenge, not in the principle and motive of condemnation, but in the material part of condemnation, so God assists in that action of a man wherein sin is placed, but not in that which is the formal reason of sin, which is a privation of some perfection the action ought morally to have.

(3) Causality of an action as such vs causality of the sinfulness of that action.

It will appear further in this, that hence it follows that the action and the viciousness of the action may have two distinct causes. That may be a cause of the one that is not the cause of the other, and hath no hand in the producing of it. God concurs to the act of the mind as it counsels, and to the external action upon that counsel, as he preserves the faculty, and gives strength to the mind to consult, and the other parts to execute; yet he is not in the least tainted with the viciousness of the action.

Though the action be from God as a concurrent cause, yet the ill quality of the action is solely from the creature with whom God concurs. The sun and the earth concur to the production of all the plants that are formed in the womb of the one and midwived by the other. The sun distributes heat, and the earth communicates sap; it is the same heat dispersed by the one, and the same juice bestowed by the other. It hath not a sweet juice for one and a sour juice for another. This general influx of the sun and earth is not the immediate cause that one plant is poisonous and another wholesome, but the sap of the earth is turned by the nature and quality of each plant. If there were not such an influx of the sun and earth, no plant could exert that poison which is in its nature; but yet the sun and earth are not the cause of that poison which is in the nature of the plant. If God did not concur to the motions of men, there could be no sinful action, because there could be no action at all. Yet this concurrence is not the cause of that venom that is in the action, which ariseth from the corrupt nature of the creature, any more than the sun and earth are the cause of the poison of the plant, which is purely the effect of its own nature upon that general influx of the sun and earth.

The influence of God pierceth through all subjects, but the action of man done by that influence is vitiated according to the nature of its own corruption. As the sun equally shines through all the quarrels in the window; if the glass be bright and clear, there is a pure splendour; if it be red or green, the splendour is from the sun, but the discolouring of that light upon the wall is from the quality of the glass.

But to be yet plainer, the soul is the image of God, and by the acts of the soul we may come to the knowledge of the acts of God. The soul gives motion to the body and every member of it, and no member could move without a concurrent virtue of the soul. If a member be paralytic or gouty, whatsoever motion that gouty member hath is derived to it from the soul. But the goutiness of the member was not the act of the soul, but the fruit of ill humours in the body. The lameness of the member and the motion of the member have two distinct causes—the motion is from one cause, and the ill motion from another. As the member could not move irregularly without some ill humour or cause of that distemper, so it could not move at all without the activity of the soul.

So though God concur to the act of understanding, willing, and execution, why can he not be as free from the irregularity in all those as the soul is free from the irregularity of the motion of the body, while it is the cause of the motion itself? There are two illustrations generally used in this case that are not unfit: the motion of the pen in writing is from the hand that holds it, but the blurs by the pen are from some fault in the pen itself; and the music of the instrument is from the hand that touches it, but the jarring from the faultiness of the strings; both are the causes of the motion of the pen and strings, but not the blurs or jarrings.

(4) Liberty and contingency of second causes established.

It is very congruous to the wisdom of God, to move his creatures according to their particular natures, but this motion makes him not the cause of sin. Had our innocent nature continued, God had moved us according to that innocent nature. But when the state was changed for a corrupt one, God must either forbear all concourse, and so annihilate the world, or move us according to that nature he finds in us. If he had overthrown the world upon the entrance of sin, and created another upon the same terms, sin might have as soon defaced his second work, as it did the first, and then it would follow that God would have been alway building and demolishing. It was not fit for God to cease from acting as a wise governor of his creature, because man did cease from his loyalty as a subject. Is it not more agreeable to God's wisdom as a governor, to concur with his creature according to his nature, than to deny his concurrence upon every evil determination of the creature! God concurred with Adam's mutable nature in his first act of sin; he concurred to the act, and left him to his mutability. If Adam had put out his hand to eat of any other unforbidden fruit, God would have supported his natural faculty then, and concurred with him in his motion.

When Adam would put out his hand to take the forbidden fruit, God concurred to that natural action, but left him to the choice of the object, and to the use of his mutable nature. And when man became apostate, God concurs with him according to that condition wherein he found him, and cannot move him otherwise, unless he should alter that nature man had contracted. God moving the creature as he found him, is no cause of the ill motion of the creature—as when a wheel is broken the space of a foot, it cannot but move ill in that part till it be mended. He that moves it, uses the same motion (as it is his act) which he would have done had the wheel been sound. So the motion is good in the mover, but bad in the subject. It is not the fault of him that moves it, but the fault of that wheel that is moved, whose breaches came by some other cause. A man doth not lay aside his watch for some irregularity, as long as it is capable of motion, but winds it up. Why should God cease from concurring with his creature in its vital operations and other actions of his will because there was a flaw contracted in that nature that came right and true out of his hand? And as he that winds up his disordered watch is in the same manner the cause of its motion then, as he was when it was regular, yet by that act of his, he is not the cause of the false motion of it, but that is from the deficiency of some part of the watch itself. So though God concurs to that action of the creature, whereby the wickedness of the heart is drawn out, yet is not God therefore as unholy as the heart.

(5) God's intention vs man's intention.

God hath one end in his concurrence, and man another in his action. So that there is a righteous, and often a gracious end in God, when there is a base and unworthy end in man. God concurs to the substance of the act; man produceth the circumstance of the act, whereby it is evil. God orders both the action wherein he concurs, and the sinfulness over which he presides, as a governor, to his own ends. In Joseph's case, man was sinful, and God merciful; his brethren acted envy, and God designed mercy (Gen. 45:4-5). They would be rid of him as an eyesore, and God concurred with their action to make him their preserver: "Ye thought evil against me, but God meant it unto good" (Gen. 50:20). God concurred to Judas his action of betraying our Saviour; he supported his nature while he contracted with the priests, and supported his members while he was their guide to apprehend him. God's end was the manifestation of his choicest love to man, and Judas his end was the gratification of his own covetousness. The Assyrian did a divine work against Jerusalem, but not with a divine end (Isa. 10:5-7). He had a mind to enlarge his empire, enrich his coffers with the spoil, and gain the title of a conqueror; he is desirous to invade his neighbours, and God employs him to punish his rebels; but "he means not so, nor doth his heart think so" (Isa. 10:7). He intended not as God intended.

The ax doth not think what the carpenter intends to do with it. But God used the rapine of an ambitious nature as an instrument of his justice. As the exposing malefactors to wild beasts was an ancient punishment, whereby the magistrate intended the execution of justice, and to that purpose used the natural fierceness of the beasts to an end different from what those ravaging creatures aimed at, God concurred with Satan in spoiling Job of his goods, and scarifying his body; God gave Satan license to do it, and Job acknowledges it to be God's act (Job. 1:12, 21). But their ends were different; God concurred with Satan for the clearing the integrity of his servant, when Satan aimed at nothing but the provoking him to curse his Creator.

The physician applies leeches to suck the superfluous blood, but the leeches suck to glut themselves, without any regard to the intention of the physician, and the welfare of the patient. In the same act where men intend to hurt, God intends to correct; so that his concurrence is in a holy manner, while men commit unrighteous actions. A judge commands the executioner to execute the sentence of death which he hath justly pronounced against a malefactor, and admonisheth him to do it out of love to justice; the executioner hath the authority of the judge for his commission, and the protection of the judge for his security. The judge stands by to countenance and secure him in the doing of it; but if the executioner hath not the same intention as the judge, viz., a love to justice in the performance of his office, but a private hatred to the offender, the judge, though he commanded the fact of the executioner, yet did not command this error of his in it; and though he protects him in the fact, yet he owns not his corrupt disposition in him in the doing of what was enjoined him, as any act of his own.

Conclusion.

To conclude this, since the creature cannot act without God, cannot lift up a hand, or move his tongue, without God's preserving and upholding the faculty and preserving the power of action, and preserving every member of the body in its actual motion, and in every circumstance of its motion, we must necessarily suppose God to have such a way of concurrence as doth not intrench upon his holiness. We must not equal the creature to God, by denying its dependence on him, nor must we imagine such a concurrence to the fulness of an act, as stains the divine purity, which is, I think, sufficiently salved by distinguishing the matter of the act, from the evil adhering to it. For since all evil is founded in some good, the evil is distinguishable from the good, and the deformity of the action from the action itself, which as it is a created act, hath a dependence on the will and influence of God, and as it is a sinful act, is the product of the will of the creature.

Chapter Five

Theodicy & God's Restraining Grace

P rop. 7. The holiness of God is not blemished by withdrawing his grace from a sinful creature, whereby he falls into more sin. That God withdraws his grace from men, and gives them up sometimes to the fury of their lusts, is as clear in Scripture as anything: "Yet the Lord hath not given you a heart to perceive, and eyes to see, and ears to hear" (Deut. 29:4). Judas was delivered to Satan after the sop, and put into his power for despising former admonitions. He often leaves the reins to the devil, that he may use what efficacy he can in those that have offended the majesty of God; he withholds further influences of grace, or withdraws what before he had granted them. Thus he withheld that grace from the sons of Eli, that might have made their father's pious admonitions effectual to them: "They hearkened not to the voice of their father, because the Lord would slay them." (1 Sam. 2:25). He gave grace to Eli to reprove them, and withheld that grace from them which might have enabled them, against their natural corruption and obstinacy, to receive that reproof. But the holiness of God is not blemished by this:

1. God's withholding of his softening grace.

Because the act of God in this is only negative. Thus God is said to harden men, not by positive hardening, or working anything in the creature, but by not working, not softening, leaving a man to the hardness of his own heart, whereby it is unavoidable, by the depravation of man's nature, and the fury of his passions, but that he should be further hardened, and "increase unto more ungodliness" as the expression is in 2 Timothy 2:16. As a man is said to give another his life, when he doth not take it away when it lay at his mercy, so God is said to harden a man when he doth not mollify him when it was in his power, and inwardly quicken him with that grace whereby he might infallibly avoid any further provoking of him. God is said to harden men, when he removes not from them the incentives to sin, curbs not those principles which are ready to comply with those incentives, withdraws the common assistances of his grace, concurs not with counsels and admonitions to make them effectual, flasheth not in the convincing light which he darted upon them before.

If hardness follows upon God's withholding his softening grace, it is not from any positive act of God, but from the natural hardness of man. If you put fire near to wax or resin, both will melt; but when the fire is removed, they return to their natural quality of hardness and brittleness. The positive act of the fire is to melt and soften, and the softness of the rosin is to be ascribed to that, but the hardness is from the resin itself, wherein the fire hath no influence, but only a negative act by a removal of it; so when God hardens a man, he only leaves him to that stony heart which he derived from Adam, and brought with him into the world. All men's understandings being blinded, and their wills perverted in Adam, God's withdrawing his grace is but a leaving them to their natural pravity, which is the cause of their further sinning, and not God's removal of that special light he before afforded them, or restraint he held over them. As when God withdraws his preserving power from the creature, he is not the *efficient*, but *deficient*, cause of the creature's destruction; so in this case, God only ceaseth to bind and dam up that sin which else would break out.

2. Man's corruption causes his own hardness of heart.

The whole positive cause of this hardness is from man's corruption. God infuseth not any sin into his creatures, but forbears to infuse his grace and restrain their lusts, which upon the removal of his grace work impetuously. God only gives them up to that which he knows will work strongly in their hearts. And therefore the apostle wipes off from God any positive act in that uncleanness the heathens were given up to ("Wherefore God gave them up to uncleanness, through the lusts of their own hearts," Rom. 1:24, and God gave them up to "vile affections," Rom. 1:26, but they were their own affections, none of God's inspiring), but adding, through the lusts of their own hearts. God's giving them up was the logical cause, or a cause by way of argument; their own lusts were the true and natural cause; their own they were before they were given up to them, and belonging to none as the author, but themselves after they were given up to them. The lust in the heart, and the temptation without, easily close and mix interests with one another; as the fire in a coal pit will with the fuel, if the streams derived into it for the quenching it be dammed up; the natural passions will run to a temptation, as the waters of a river tumble towards the sea. When a man that hath bridled in a high-mettled horse from running out, gives him the reins, or a huntsman takes off the string that held the dog, and lets him run after the hare, are they the immediate cause of the motion of the one or the other? No; but the mettle and strength of the horse, and the natural inclination of the hound, both which are left to their own motions to pursue their own natural instincts.

Man doth as naturally tend to sin as a stone to the center, or as a weighty thing inclines to a motion to the earth; it is from the propension of man's nature that he "drinks up iniquity like water" (Job 15:16). God doth no more when he leaves a man to sin, by taking away the hedge which stopped him, but leave him to his natural inclination. As a man that breaks up a dam he hath placed, leaves the stream to run in their natural channel, or one that takes away a prop from a stone to let it fall, leaves it only to that nature which inclines it to a descent, both have their motion from their own nature, and man his sin from his own corruption. The withdrawing the sunbeams is not the cause of darkness, but the shadiness of the earth; nor is the departure of the sun the cause of winter, but the coldness of the air and earth, which was tempered and beaten back into the bowels of the earth by the vigour of the sun, upon whose departure they return to their natural state. The sun only leaves the earth and air as it found them at the beginning of the spring, or the beginning of the day.

If God do not give a man grace to melt him, yet he cannot be said to communicate to him that nature which hardens him, which man hath from himself. As God was not the cause of the first sin of Adam, which was the root of all other, so he is not the cause of the following sins, which as branches spring from that root; man's free will was the cause of the first sin, and the corruption of his nature by it the cause of all succeeding sins. God doth not immediately harden any man, but doth propose those things from whence the natural vice of man takes an occasion to strengthen and nourish itself. Hence God is said to "harden Pharaoh's heart" (Exod. 7:13), by concurring with the magicians in turning their rods into serpents, which stiffened his heart against Moses, conceiving him by reason of that to have no more power than other men, and was an occasion of his further hardening; and Pharaoh is said to harden himself (Exod. 8:32); that is, in regard of his own natural passion.

3. God withdraws from sinful man.

God is holy and righteous, because he doth not withdraw from man till man deserts him. To say that God withdrew that grace from Adam, which he had afforded him in creation, or anything that was due to him, till he had abused the gifts of God, and turned them to an end contrary to that of creation, would be a reflection upon the divine holiness. God was first deserted by man before man was deserted by God, and man doth first contemn and abuse the common grace of God, and those relics of natural light that "enlighten every man that comes into the world" (John 1:9) before God leaves him to the hurry of his own passions. Ephraim was first "joined to idols," before God pronounced the fatal sentence, "Let him alone" (Hosea 4:17). And the heathens first "changed the glory of the incorruptible God" (Rom. 1:23-24), before God withdrew his common grace from the corrupted creature, and they first "serve the creature more than the Creator," before the Creator gave them up to the slavish chains of their vile affections (Rom. 1:25-26). Israel first cast off God before God cast off them, but then "he gave them up to their own heart's lusts, and they walked in their own counsels" (Ps. 81:11-12).

Since sin entered into the world by the fall of Adam, and the blood of all his posterity was tainted, man cannot do anything that is formally good; not for want of faculties, but for the want of a righteous habit in those faculties, especially in the will; yet God discovers himself to man in the works of his hands; he hath left in him footsteps of natural reason, he doth attend him with common motions of his Spirit, corrects him for his faults with gentle chastisements. He is near unto all in some kind of instructions; he puts many times providential bars in their way of sinning, but when they will rush into it "as the horse into the battle," when they will rebel against the light, God doth often leave them to their own course, sentence "him that is filthy to be filthy still" (Rev. 22:11), which is a righteous act of God, as he is rector and governor of the world. Man's not receiving, or not improving what God gives, is the cause of God's not giving further, or taking away his own, which before he had bestowed.

This is so far from being repugnant to the holiness and righteousness of God, that it is rather a commendable act of his holiness and righteousness, as the rector of the world, not to let those gifts continue in the hand of a man who abuses them contrary to his glory. Who will blame a father, that after all the good counsels he hath given his son to reclaim him, all the corrections he hath inflicted on him for his irregular practice, leaves him to his own courses, and withdraws those assistances which he scoffed at and turned the deaf ear unto? Or who will blame the physician for deserting the patient who rejects his counsel, will not follow his prescriptions, but dasheth his physic against the wall? No man will blame him, no man will say that he is the cause of the patient's death; but the true cause is the fury of the distemper, and the obstinacy of the diseased person, to which the physician left him. And who can justly blame God in this case, who yet never denied supplies of grace to any that sincerely sought it at his hands? and what man is there that lies under a hardness, but first was guilty of very provoking sins? What unholiness is it to deprive men of those assistances because of their sin, and afterwards to direct those counsels and practices of theirs which he hath justly given them up unto, to serve the ends of his own glory in his own methods?

4. God is not obligated to be gracious.

Which will appear further by considering that God is not obliged to continue his grace to them. It was at his liberty whether he would give any renewing grace to Adam after his fall, or to any of his posterity; he was at his own liberty to withhold it or communicate it; but if he were under any obligation then, surely he must be under less now, since the multiplication of sin by his creatures; but if the obligation were none just after the fall, there is no pretense now to fasten any such obligation on God. That God had no obligation at first hath been spoken to before; he is less obliged to continue his grace after a repeated refusal, and a peremptory abuse, than he was bound to proffer it after the first apostasy.

God cannot be charged with unholiness in withdrawing his grace after we have received it, unless we can make it appear that his grace was a thing due to us, as we are his creatures, and as he is the governor of the world. What prince looks upon himself as obliged to reside in any particular place of his kingdom? But suppose he be bound to inhabit in one particular city, yet after the city rebels against him, is he bound to continue his court there, spend his revenue among rebels, endanger his own honour and security, enlarge their charter, or maintain their ancient privileges? Is it not most just and righteous for him to withdraw himself, and leave them to their own tumultuousness and sedition, whereby they should eat the fruit of their own doings? If there be an obligation on God as a governor, it would rather lie on the side of justice, to leave man to the power of the devil, whom he courted, and the prevalence of those lusts he hath so often caressed, and wrap up in a cloud all his common illuminations, and leave him destitute of all common workings of his Spirit.

Chapter Six

APPENDIX

God is Not the Author of Sin

Girolamo Zanchi *Observations on the Divine Attributes*, **4.3**
     WCF 3.1 God from all eternity did, by the most wise and holy counsel of his own will, freely and unchangeably ordain whatsoever comes to pass (Rom 9:15, 18; 11:33; Eph 1:11; Heb 6:17); yet so as thereby neither is God the author of sin (James 1:13, 17; 1 John 1:5), nor is violence offered to the will of the creatures, nor is the liberty or contingency of **second causes** taken away, but rather established (Prov 16:33; Mat 17:12; John 19:11; Acts 2:23; 4:27-28).

WCF 5.2 Although in relation to the foreknowledge and decree of God, **the first cause**, all things come to pass immutably and infallibly (Acts 2:23), yet by the same providence he ordereth them to fall out, according to the nature of **second causes**, either necessarily, freely, or contingently (Gen 8:22; Exod 21:13 with Deut 19:5; 1 Kings 22:28, 34; Isa 10:6-7; Jer 31:35).

God, as the primary and efficient cause of all things, is not only the Author of those actions done by His elect as actions, but also as they are good actions, whereas, on the other hand, though He may be said to be the Author of all the actions done by the wicked, yet He is not the Author of them in a moral and compound sense as they are sinful; but physically, simply and *sensu diviso*[1] as they are mere actions, abstractedly from all consideration of the goodness or badness of them.

Although there is no action whatever which is not in some sense either good or bad, yet we can easily conceive of an action, purely as such, without adverting to the quality of it, so that the distinction between an action itself and its denomination of good or evil is very obvious and natural.

In and by the elect, therefore, God not only produces works and actions through His almighty power, but likewise, through the salutary influences of His Spirit, first makes their persons good, and then their actions so too; but, in and by the reprobate, He produces actions by His power alone, which actions, as neither issuing from faith nor being wrought with a view to the Divine glory, nor done in the manner prescribed by the Divine Word, are, on these accounts, properly denominated evil. Hence we see that God does not, immediately and *per se*, infuse iniquity into the wicked; but, as Luther expresses it, powerfully excites them to action, and withholds those gracious influences of His Spirit, without which every action is necessarily evil.

---

1. [1] *sensus divisus*: the divided sense; i.e. the meaning of a word or idea in itself apart from its general relation to other words of a text; the opposite of *sensus compositus*. *Sensus compositus*: composite sense; also *sensus literalis compositus*: composite or compounded literal sense; as distinguished from a divided or isolated sense. (Richard Muller, *Dictionary of Latin and Greek Theological Terms*, 1st ed., p. 279).

That God either directly or remotely excites bad men as well as good ones to action cannot be denied by any but Atheists, or by those who carry their notions of free-will and human independency so high as to exclude the Deity from all actual operation in and among His creatures, which is little short of Atheism. Every work performed, whether good or evil, is done in strength and by the power derived immediately from God Himself, *"in whom all men live, move, and have their being"* (Acts 17:28). As, at first, without Him was not anything made which was made, so, now, without Him is not anything done which is done. We have no power or faculty, whether corporal or intellectual, but what we received from God, subsists by Him, and is exercised in subserviency to His will and appointment. It is He who created, preserves, actuates and directs all things. But it by no means follows, from these premises, that God is therefore the cause of sin, for sin is nothing but ἀνομία, illegality, want of conformity to the Divine law (1 John 3:4), a mere privation of rectitude; consequently, being itself a thing purely negative, it can have no positive or efficient cause, but only a negative and deficient one, as several learned men have observed.

Every action, as such, is undoubtedly good, it being an actual exertion of those operative powers given us by God for that very end; God therefore may be the Author of all actions (as He undoubtedly is), and yet not be the Author of evil. An action is constituted evil three ways—by proceeding from a wrong principle, by being directed to a wrong end, and by being done in a wrong manner. Now, though God, as we have said, is the efficient cause of our actions as actions, yet, if these actions commence sinful, that sinfulness arises from ourselves. Suppose a boy, who knows not how to write, has his hand guided by his master and nevertheless makes false letters, quite unlike the copy set him, though his preceptor, who guides his hand, is the cause of his writing at all, yet his own ignorance and unskillfulness are the cause of his writing so badly. Just so, God is the supreme Author of our action, abstractedly taken, but our own vitiosity is the cause of our acting amiss.

www.ingramcontent.com/pod-product-compliance
Lightning Source LLC
Chambersburg PA
CBHW051335120626
46547CB00016B/2558